BEHIND THE BRAND

SEGA

T0023697

BY SARA GREEN

BELLWETHER MEDIA • MINNEAPOLIS, MN

Blastoff! Discovery launches a new mission: reading to learn. Filled with facts and features, each book offers you an exciting new world to explore!

BLASTOFF! UNIVERSE

BLASTOFF! DISCOVERY

GRADE K

GRADES 1-3

GRADE 4

This edition first published in 2024 by Bellwether Media, Inc.

No part of this publication may be reproduced in whole or in part without written permission of the publisher.
For information regarding permission, write to Bellwether Media, Inc.,
Attention: Permissions Department,
6012 Blue Circle Drive, Minnetonka, MN 55343.

Library of Congress Cataloging-in-Publication Data

Names: Green, Sara, 1964- author.
Title: Sega / Sara Green.
Description: Minneapolis, MN : Bellwether Media, Inc., 2024. | Series: Behind the brand | Includes bibliographical references and index. | Audience: Ages 7-13 | Audience: Grades 4-6 | Summary: "Engaging images accompany information about Sega. The combination of high-interest subject matter and narrative text is intended for students in grades 3 through 8"–Provided by publisher.
Identifiers: LCCN 2023045258 (print) | LCCN 2023045259 (ebook) | ISBN 9798886878103 (library binding) | ISBN 9798886879568 (paperback) | ISBN 9798886879049 (ebook)
Subjects: LCSH: Sega of America (Firm)–History–Juvenile literature. | Sonic the Hedgehog (Video game)–Juvenile literature. | Sega Genesis video games–Juvenile literature. | Sega Dreamcast video games–History. | Sega Saturn video games–History.
Classification: LCC GV1469.325 .G74 2024 (print) | LCC GV1469.325 (ebook) | DDC 794.8–dc23/eng/20230927
LC record available at https://lccn.loc.gov/2023045258
LC ebook record available at https://lccn.loc.gov/2023045259

Editor: Betsy Rathburn   Designer: Andrea Schneider

Printed in the United States of America, North Mankato, MN.

TABLE OF

CONTENTS

A HEROIC HEDGEHOG!

SONIC FRONTIERS

THE BLUE BLUR

Sonic is called the Blue Blur because of his blue fur and fast running speed. He often curls into a ball to charge through his enemies!

A boy plays as Sonic the Hedgehog in *Sonic Frontiers*. He is ready to run! As the game begins, Sonic and his friends are pulled through a wormhole. Sonic lands in Starfall Islands. But his friends are trapped in Cyber Space!

To free them, Sonic must collect the Chaos Emeralds hidden in the islands. Along the way, he must solve puzzles and battle robot enemies such as Soldiers, Guardians, and Titans. Will Sonic's skill and supersonic speed be enough to defeat them? This exciting **3D** game is full of adventure. It is one of many games made by Sega!

KRONOS ISLAND
STARFALL ISLANDS

GUARDIAN

STARTING SEGA

SEGA ARCADE
TOKYO, JAPAN

SEGA GAME GEAR

Sega is a company that makes video games. Its **headquarters** is in Tokyo, Japan. Sega also has offices in the United States and Europe.

FAMILY FUN!

Sega has made dozens of arcade games. *Sonic Sports Basketball*, *Polar Slide*, and *Tetris Giant* are a few popular ones!

Sega makes games for many popular **consoles**. Sega games can also be played on computers and **mobile** devices. Sega is best known for its Sonic the Hedgehog games. But it makes many other popular video games, too! Many people enjoy playing Sega **arcade** games. People can collect Sega toys, clothing, and other items. They can even watch movies based on their favorite games!

SEGA HEADQUARTERS

TOKYO, JAPAN

ASIA

Sega started in 1940 in Hawaii as a company called Standard Games. It was founded by Irving Bromberg, Martin Bromley, and James Humpert. Standard Games sold coin-operated **gambling** machines to U.S. military bases. The company's name later changed to Service Games because of its ties to military service.

COIN-OPERATED
GAMBLING MACHINES

SEGA HEADQUARTERS
TOKYO, JAPAN

In 1951, the U.S. government passed a new law.
It banned gambling machines on military bases in
the U.S. As a result, the company moved to Japan in
1952. There, it was renamed Service Games of Japan.

THE SEGA NAME

The name *Sega* comes from the first
two letters of "Service" and "Games."

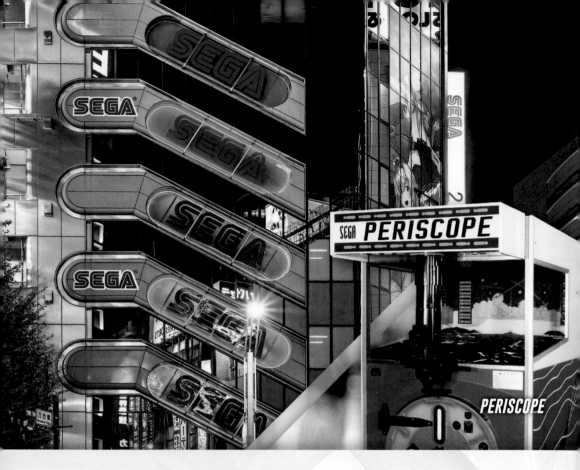

PERISCOPE

Around the same time, another entertainment company called Rosen **Enterprises** was also finding success in Japan. The company **imported** photo booths and game machines from the U.S. In 1965, Service Games of Japan and Rosen Enterprises **merged**. The new company was called Sega Enterprises, or Sega.

EARLY HITS

Drivemobile and *Motopolo* were popular Sega arcade games that came out in the 1960s.

Sega released its first arcade game in Japan in 1966. It was a submarine battle game called *Periscope*. It was an instant hit! Soon, Sega began selling and shipping *Periscope* machines to the U.S. They were set up in places such as malls and department stores. American gamers loved *Periscope*!

SEGA TIMELINE

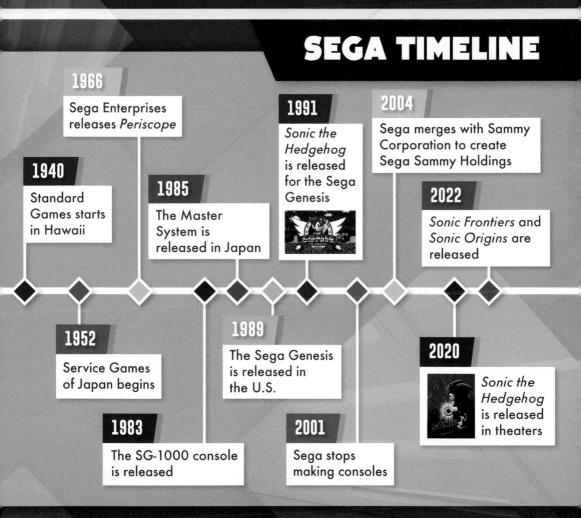

1966
Sega Enterprises releases *Periscope*

1940
Standard Games starts in Hawaii

1985
The Master System is released in Japan

1991
Sonic the Hedgehog is released for the Sega Genesis

2004
Sega merges with Sammy Corporation to create Sega Sammy Holdings

2022
Sonic Frontiers and *Sonic Origins* are released

1952
Service Games of Japan begins

1989
The Sega Genesis is released in the U.S.

2020
Sonic the Hedgehog is released in theaters

1983
The SG-1000 console is released

2001
Sega stops making consoles

Sega continued to grow. The company released its first console, the SG-1000, in the early 1980s. But the console was not successful. Sales were low. In the mid-1980s, Sega released a new console called the Master System.

MASTER SYSTEM

Now, there are no limits. SEGA®

SG-1000

NINTENDO CONSOLE

TONKA TOY

The Master System helped Sega compete with other game companies such as Nintendo and Atari. It did well in Europe and South America. But it never gained a strong fan base in the U.S. In 1988, Sega partnered with Tonka, a toy **manufacturer**, to boost sales. But this did not work. Sega stopped making the Master System in 1992.

ALEX KIDD IN THE
ENCHANTED CASTLE

16-BIT

    Despite this setback, Sega did not give up. The company
quickly released another console called the Mega Drive.
It launched in Japan in 1988. A year later, Sega released
the console in the U.S. Its name was changed to the
Genesis for the North American market.

The Genesis was a more advanced console. Its graphics featured more color and details than previous consoles. It also offered more games. Early Genesis games such as *Joe Montana Football* and *Alex Kidd in the Enchanted Castle* drew in players. But Sega still faced competition from Nintendo.

POPULAR GENESIS GAMES

OUT RUN
Year Released in the U.S.: 1991

TOEJAM & EARL
Year Released in the U.S.: 1991

SONIC THE HEDGEHOG
Year Released in the U.S.: 1991

ECCO THE DOLPHIN
Year Released in the U.S.: 1992

DR. ROBOTNIK'S MEAN BEAN MACHINE
Year Released in the U.S.: 1993

SONIC & KNUCKLES
Year Released in the U.S.: 1994

Sega was determined to beat Nintendo.
Company leaders decided to invent a **mascot** to
compete with Mario, Nintendo's mascot. Naoto
Ohshima, Yuji Naka, and Hirokazu Yasuhara
created a blue hedgehog named Sonic. This
daredevil could run at superfast speeds!

NAOTO OHSHIMA

BORN
February 26, 1964,
in Osaka, Japan

ROLE
Artist and video
game designer

ACCOMPLISHMENTS

Designed the characters
Sonic the Hedgehog and
Dr. Robotnik from the Sonic the
Hedgehog video game series

SONIC THE
HEDGEHOG GAME

SONIC THE
HEDGEHOG

In 1991, Sega launched a game called *Sonic the Hedgehog*. Gamers began to zoom across the landscape as Sonic. They had to defeat Dr. Robotnik and collect Chaos Emeralds to win the game. *Sonic the Hedgehog* was a smash hit. Sega began bundling the game with Genesis consoles. The demand for Genesis consoles skyrocketed. By December 1991, Sega had the lead in console sales!

AHEAD OF ITS TIME

The Dreamcast was one of the first consoles that let users play games online!

DREAMCAST

Sega was confident it could make more hit consoles. However, the Sega Saturn, released in Japan in 1994, was unsuccessful. Four years later, Sega released the Dreamcast. It was more powerful than the Saturn. Its popular games included *Sonic Adventure* and *NFL 2K*. Sega sold more than 9 million Dreamcasts!

Despite the strong start, Dreamcast sales soon dropped. The company did a poor job **advertising** the console. Its design annoyed many gamers. The Dreamcast also faced stiff competition from other consoles. In 2001, Sega stopped making consoles. It decided to focus on making games instead.

NFL 2K

SONIC
ADVENTURE

More changes followed. In 2004, Sega merged with a Japanese company called Sammy. They created a new company called Sega Sammy Holdings.

SONIC THE HEDGEHOG CHARACTERS

SONIC
First Appearance:
Sonic the Hedgehog
Year: 1991

DR. ROBOTNIK
First Appearance:
Sonic the Hedgehog
Year: 1991

TAILS
First Appearance:
Sonic the Hedgehog 2
Year: 1992

AMY ROSE
First Appearance:
Sonic CD
Year: 1993

METAL SONIC
First Appearance:
Sonic CD
Year: 1993

KNUCKLES
First Appearance:
Sonic the Hedgehog 3
Year: 1994

SUPER MONKEY BALL

SEGA RALLY 2006

Under new leadership, Sega began releasing games for Nintendo, PlayStation, and Xbox consoles. Early games included *Football Manager: 2006*, *Charlotte's Web*, and *Sega Rally 2006*. The company also continued to make popular Sonic games such as *Sonic Rush* and *Shadow the Hedgehog*. A **role-playing game** called *Sonic Chronicles: The Dark Brotherhood* was released in 2008. That year, Sega also launched *Super Monkey Ball* as a mobile **app**. The game was an instant hit!

SPEEDING AHEAD

PEOPLE PLAYING SONIC FRONTIERS

A HAPPY HEDGEHOG!

Over time, more than 1 billion Sonic the Hedgehog games have been sold!

Today, people around the world play Sega games every day. They are available on the world's most popular consoles. Sega also remade its old consoles. The Sega Genesis Mini launched in 2019, and the Genesis Mini 2 was released in 2022. They come loaded with dozens of classic Sega games!

Sega continues to bring new fans to the **brand** with Sonic. Two games released in 2022 add extra fun to the series. *Sonic Origins* brings four Sonic games together into one fun game. *Sonic Frontiers* allows gamers to roam freely through its world!

TOP-SELLING SONIC GAMES

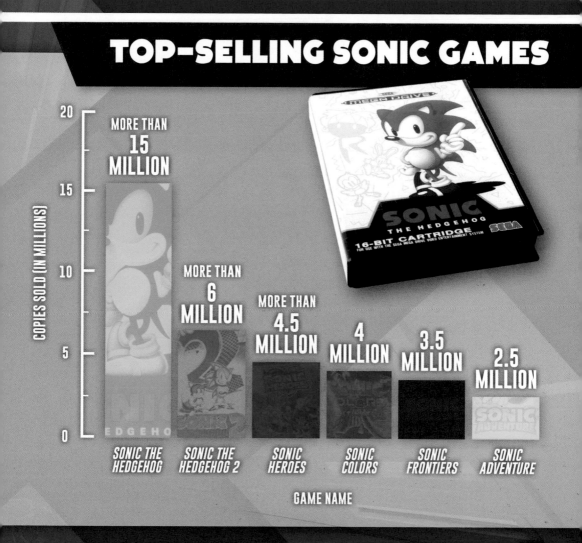

COPIES SOLD (IN MILLIONS)

20

15

10

5

0

MORE THAN
15 MILLION

MORE THAN
6 MILLION

MORE THAN
4.5 MILLION

4 MILLION

3.5 MILLION

2.5 MILLION

SONIC THE HEDGEHOG

SONIC THE HEDGEHOG 2

SONIC HEROES

SONIC COLORS

SONIC FRONTIERS

SONIC ADVENTURE

GAME NAME

SONIC THE HEDGEHOG
MOVIE

SONIC PRIME

Sonic Prime is a popular series on Netflix. Sonic races through many universes to save his friends and the world!

Sonic can also be seen on the big screen. *Sonic the Hedgehog* was released in 2020. It was one of the most successful video game movies ever! In 2022, *Sonic the Hedgehog 2* was another huge hit!

Other Sega series also enjoy success. Many gamers play *Total War* and *Football Manager 2023*. Fans can look forward to exciting new games, too. In 2026, Sega plans to release a "Super Game" that includes favorite characters from many different games. In 2023, Sega bought Rovio Entertainment, known for the mobile game *Angry Birds*. Together, they plan to make Sega mobile games!

ANGRY BIRDS

ANGRY BIRDS

SONIC THE HEDGEHOG 2
MOVIE

SUPPORTING OTHERS

JAPAN AFTER AN
EARTHQUAKE IN 2011

Sega makes a difference in people's lives! Since 2009, Sega has sent 2,825 books to children living in conflict areas in Asia. Between 2011 and 2015, 465 Sega employees worked to help communities in Japan recover from an earthquake.

Sega also supports equal rights for all people. In 2021, the company promised to give money to organizations that fight **racism**. In 2022, Sega employees raised around $22,000 to support the Mermaids **charity**. Sega also matches money given by employees to organizations that support women's health.

465 SEGA EMPLOYEES WORKED
TO HELP WITH EARTHQUAKE RECOVERY BETWEEN 2011 AND 2015

EMPLOYEES RAISED
$22,000
TO SUPPORT THE MERMAIDS CHARITY
IN 2022

2,825 BOOKS
DONATED SINCE 2009

MORE FUN WITH SEGA!

VIDEO GAME CONVENTION

SONIC LEGO MINIFIGURE

SONIC FRONTIER

Sega fans enjoy the brand in many ways. People can use LEGO's Sonic sets to recreate their favorite Sonic levels. Sonic is also on Roblox. Gamers dash across a 3D world in *Sonic Speed Simulator*!

FAN PARTICIPATION

Sonic fans helped make the game *Sonic Mania*! They were developers known for making Sonic fan games. Sega hired them to make an official game!

Conventions are another fun way for fans to connect. Sonic Revolution is held every summer in California. This event includes interviews with game developers and artists. Fans can enter contests and meet people involved in creating games. Sega entertains and delights people across the globe!

SONIC REVOLUTION

WHAT IT IS

A convention where fans can meet artists and content creators in the Sonic community

WHEN IT HAPPENS Yearly

FIRST HAPPENED 2014

WHERE IT HAPPENS

California and online

GLOSSARY

3D—showing length, height, and depth

advertising—announcing or promoting something to get people to buy it

app—a program such as a game or internet browser; an app is also called an application.

arcade—related to places where people can play coin-operated games

brand—a category of products all made by the same company

charity—an organization that helps others in need

consoles—electronic devices for playing video games

conventions—events where fans of a subject meet

enterprises—business organizations

gambling—related to playing games of chance for money

graphics—art such as illustrations or designs

headquarters—a company's main office

imported—brought products from one country to another

manufacturer—a company that makes items for people to use

mascot—an animal or object used as a symbol by a group or company

merged—joined together

mobile—small enough to be easily carried

racism—when people are treated unfairly based on their skin color

role-playing game—a game in which players take on the roles of characters to complete the game

TO LEARN MORE

AT THE LIBRARY

Dulling, Kaitlyn. *Power On: The History of Gaming*. Greensboro, N.C.: Rourke Educational Media, 2022.

Rusick, Jessica. *Sonic the Hedgehog*. Minneapolis, Minn.: Abdo Publishing, 2022.

Schwartz, Heather E. *The History of Gaming*. Mankato, Minn.: Capstone Press, 2020.

ON THE WEB

FACTSURFER

Factsurfer.com gives you a safe, fun way to find more information.

1. Go to www.factsurfer.com.

2. Enter "Sega" into the search box and click 🔍.

3. Select your book cover to see a list of related content.

INDEX

The images in this book are reproduced through the courtesy of: minegame30, front cover (Sonic the Hedgehog); Thoaaa, front cover (Dr. Robotnik); AntMan3001, front cover (Tails); Marc Tielemans/ Alamy, front cover (video games), p. 23 (*Sonic the Hedgehog 2*); Evan-Amos/ Wikipedia, front cover (Sega Genesis), pp. 12 (SG-1000), 14 (Mega Drive), 18 (Dreamcast); Justin Towell/ Alamy, front cover (background video games); Robtek, pp. 2-3; joe mama, p. 3; JJFarq, pp. 4-5; ZUMA Press Inc/ Alamy, p. 4 (*Sonic Frontiers*); RoseStudio, pp. 4 (Blue Blur), 11 (1991); Betsy Rathburn, p. 5 (Guardian, Kronos Island); KhunO, p. 6 (Sega arcade); Christos Film, p. 6 (Game Gear); ackats, p. 6 (arcade game); apiguide, p. 7 (Tokyo background); Rodw/ Wikipedia, p. 8 (Akonnchiroll, p. 9 (Sega headquarters); Savvapanf Photo, p. 9 (Sega sign); Kuremo, p. 10; Sega, p. 10 (*Periscope, Drivemobile*); TCD/Prod.DB/ Alamy, p. 11 (2020); Valentin Kozin, p. 12 (Master System); robtek, p. 13 (Nintendo console); The Image Party, p. 13 (Tonka toy); Vanessa Sanches, p. 14 (*Alex Kidd in the Enchanted Castle*); vonguard, p. 15 (*Out Run, ToeJam & Earl, Sonic the Hedgehog, Ecco the Dolphin, Dr. Robotnik's Mean Bean Machine, Sonic & Knuckles*); Game Developers Conference/ Wikipedia, p. 16 (Naoto Ohshima); ArcadeImages/ Alamy, pp. 17 (*Sonic the Hedgehog* game), 19 (*NFL 2K, Sonic Adventure*), 21 (*Super Monkey Ball*); MOHAMEDE the haryry, pp. 17 (Sonic the Hedgehog), 21 (Tails); B Christopher/ Alamy, pp. 18-19; Shutterstock, p. 20 (Sonic, Knuckles; JeremyFelan, p. 20 (Dr. Robotnik); on demand vectora 19, p. 20 (Amy Rose); nezukoofficial, p. 20 (Metal Sonic); Manuel Sagra, p. 21 (*Sega Rally 2006*); SOPA Images Limited/ Alamy, p. 22 (*Sonic Frontiers*); Sega/ Sonic Team/ Wikipedia, p. 22 (Sonic the Hedgehog); ole999/ Alamy, p. 23 (*Sonic Heroes*); Sipa USA/ Alamy, p. 23 (*Sonic Frontiers*); Ben Gingell/ Alamy, p. 23 (*Sonic the Hedgehog* cartridge); Entertainment Pictures/ Alamy, pp. 24-25 (*Sonic the Hedgehog* movie); Andrea Schneider, p. 24 (*Sonic Prime*); Paramount Pictures/ Everett Collection, p. 25 (*Sonic the Hedgehog 2* movie); Sean Locke Photography, p. 25 (*Angry Birds*); KPG-Payless, p. 26; Peerapon Boonyakiat/ SOPA Images/ AP Newsroom, p. 28 (video game convention); mini_citizens, p. 28 (LEGO minifigure); MergeIdea, p. 29 (Sonic Revolution); Panther Media GmbH/ Alamy, p. 31 (Sonic); TimZillion, p. 31 (Sega Mega Drive II).